Thy
Sea
So Great

My Galleons sail on every sea
And bring their Treasures home to me

Winfred Ernest Garrison

Thy Sea So Great

A BOOK OF VERSES

By Winfred Ernest Garrison

THE BETHANY PRESS, ST. LOUIS, MISSOURI

Distributed by Thomas C. Lothian, Melbourne,
Australia, and Auckland, New Zealand, and by
The G. R. Welch Company, Toronto, Canada

MANUFACTURED IN THE UNITED STATES OF AMERICA

Foreword

THE FIRST POEM in this book, "Thy Sea So Great," was actually written on shipboard during a storm. At such a time the sea does indeed seem very great. The sea has also another kind of greatness which suggested the use of the phrase as the title for the book. The sea can not only threaten by what seems to be a concentration of angry power on the defenseless voyager. It can also carry the inquisitive traveler, or the man with a mission, to far and strange places from which he can return with varied cargoes of sights and ideas as well as the tangible articles of trade.

The sea washes many shores of many kinds. It thunders against the rugged cliffs of Norway, pours its waves along white sandy beaches wherever they are found, and sparkles around the palm-fringed islands of the Tropics. It ministers to many ports and carries to and from them an unimaginable variety of products. What better symbol than the sea for the vast diversity of human interests and experiences, or even for those that one person can have?

5

No one person can make all possible interests and experiences his own, or would want to, but I have had my share of them. A great many years ago I designed for myself a bookplate bearing the figure of an antique vessel and, since I could not find a suitable quotation to go with it, I wrote one:

> My galleons sail on every sea
> And bring their treasures home to me.

Some of the verses contained here—especially those of religious meaning—represent personal convictions and experiences. Many others are the product of voyages of the imagination. I hold the theory that a lyric poem may be, in a sense, dramatic; that is, the author may be putting words into the mouth of an imaginary character in an imagined situation. If a certain kind of person were involved in a certain set of circumstances, he might say what the poem says. Just what kind of person and what kind of situation should be as clear as it needs to be from the poem itself. This is what I mean by a lyric poem being dramatic and not necessarily autobiographical. I personally never did "send red roses" to anyone who "wore a yellow dress," nor did I ever pause to fight a duel and kill a man between the stanzas of a serenade to a lady in a balcony, or share ownership of a "Western sea" with anyone as suggested by "Mare Nostrum," which was written in Rome.

With very few exceptions, all these poems have passed editorial scrutiny and been published in periodicals: many of the religious ones in the *Christian Century;* some in other religious weeklies; one in the last issue of the hundred-year-old *Christian Work* (but that was not what killed it, I think); nearly all the romantic and frivolous ones in the famous "Line o' Type" column of the *Chicago Tribune,* then conducted by Richard Henry Little. A few (but very few) have been included in various anthologies and, with permission, reprinted in several places and used on radio programs. Two or three that were used in my

Variations on a Theme (Bethany Press, 1964) are repeated here.

To the lyrics there are appended two compositions in another form: the text of a Christmas pageant that was performed repeatedly in the University Church of Disciples of Christ in Chicago (my homage to Fred and Ione Wise and to Jane Moore for the success of its presentation); and a one-act play concerning St. Francis of Assisi, which has never been performed but was part of a larger project in which my competent collaborator was Margueritte Harmon Bro.

W.E.G.

Contents

CHRISTMAS MESSAGES

ROMANCE, LIMITED

TRIVIALIA ET FRIVOLA

THE DUKE'S CHRISTMAS PAGEANT

IL POVERELLO

Ad Astra

THY SEA SO GREAT

Thy sea, O God, so great,
  My boat so small,
It cannot be that any happy fate
  Will me befall
Save as Thy goodness opens paths for me
Through the consuming vastness of the sea.

Thy winds, O God, so strong,
  So slight my sail.
How could I curb and bit them on the long
  And salty trail
Unless Thy love were mightier than the wrath
Of all the tempests that beset my path?

Thy world, O God, so fierce
  And I so frail.
Yet, though its arrows threaten oft to pierce
  My fragile mail,
Cities of refuge rise where dangers cease,
Sweet silences abound, and all is peace.

WHERE IS GOD?

An eagle yearned to find the air.
  He launched from his lonely crag, and rose
To heights that only the eagles dare
  Through paths that only an eagle knows.
"I know the winds, and the gales I ride,
But where, oh where is the air?" he cried.

"I am seeking the sea," said the anxious fish.
  "Here is only water, and tides, and waves.
To look on the sea is my dearest wish.
  I have searched to the depths of the ocean caves
Where creatures of scale and fin swim free,
But I cannot find the fabled sea."

And the questing soul cried, "Where is God?
  I have sought in vain to find His throne.
He dwells no more with Aaron's rod,
  With Urim or Thummim, or Tables of Stone,
On smoking altar with candles dim,
Or between the wings of the Cherubim.

"I peer where night's purple curtains part,
  And beyond the stars in the outer void.
I trace the orbits, with subtle art,
  Of sun and planet and asteroid.
No Heaven I see, nor Hell to awe,
And ever I find not God but Law.

"I have seen a swirl of cosmic dust
  Grow into a world of living men,
Who yearn and strive, because they must,
  Who struggle and fall and rise again,
And join their wills in a common plan
To do the things that are good for man.

"I have seen the martyr's radiant face;
    I have caught the smile in a mother's eye;
And Perfect Love with Perfect Grace
    I have seen as the Brother of Men passed by.
I know the path that his feet have trod,
But tell me, oh tell me—Where is God?"

RENASCENCE

(in a sixteenth-century Spanish form called a *glosa*)

Dead leaves and a sodden sky
    On a somber autumn morn.
Whatever lives must die;
    What dies shall be reborn.

Hid by God's hand in a cleft
    I have seen His glory pass by.
The flaming bush has burned out and left
    Dead leaves and a sodden sky.

The nights are as cold as hate,
    The days are as dull as scorn.
There comes no gleam, though I watch and wait,
    On a somber autumn morn.

For hope is a broken thing,
    And laughter is stilled to a sigh.
The flowers fade and the birds take wing.
    Whatever lives must die.

Yet love is stronger than death,
    As faith is sweeter than scorn.
Life cannot lose its lightest breath.
    What dies shall be reborn.

DEDICATION OF A FIREPLACE

(Scene: Winter evening in a cabin in the Indiana Dunes
on the shore of Lake Michigan)

INVOCATION

Touched by a quickening, liberating spark,
The kindled faggots leap to life, and all
The imprisoned splendor of a thousand noons
And pent-up hues of sunsets and of dawns,
Entrapped and held in the growing wood, break free
From the concentric rings that shut them in
Season by season farther from the sun.

A rush of flame in the chimney, like a choir
Of newborn angels, crimson-clad, all singing
And praising God with lifted hands and faces,
With voices jubilant and songs exultant,
Invokes His presence in this humble hut,
While incense of blue fragrant smoke arises
In curling tendrils intricately woven.

MAGNIFICAT

Now burns the fire with steadier radiance,
For now the flames no longer dance light-footed
Upon the wood, but, deeply penetrating,
Upon its dead heart feed their living glory
And turn its blackness into molten gold.

An inner glow matching the outer shining
Fills and o'erflows the silent worshiper
Before the hearth. If such a mystery
Of light and warmth can come from oaken logs,
If stolid wood can kindle to such flame,
If this rude cabin can be so transfigured
Into a temple fit for the abode
Of the blest spirits from the heavenly places,
What miracles of beauty, love, and joy
May yet be wrought from the dull stuff of life?

16

It is an hour for wonder and for worship,
For lifting up the heart to high resolve.
Magnificat—my soul doth magnify.
Sanctus, sanctus—holy be His name.
Pleni sunt coeli et terra gloria tua.

BENEDICTION

The flame has sunk. The angel choirs are gone.
The light that gilded the rough cabin walls
Has flickered out. The stealthy shadows creep
From every corner to the very hearth.
And yet what thrilling marvels still are seen
Within the glowing embers—magic caves
Of fire and ice, scintillant corridors
That open on and on to endless thoughts
Of things long past, of friends invisible,
Of all the transient loveliness of life.

Man cannot face this deepening dusk alone.
There is a groping for an unseen hand.
Found, grasped, and held! And as the last gleam dies
There comes an ecstasy of pure content,
A sense of nearness and of comradeship.

The benediction of the dying fire
Bids the adoring worshiper depart,
But not alone. For in the dark there shines
A brighter light than angels' faces gave,
And sounds a music sweeter than their song.

HERE HAVE WE SEEN THY FACE

(For last service in old church, sung to Schubert's *Ave Maria*)

Here have we seen Thy face,
　　Father and Friend.
Here have we worshiped at Thy altar.
Here hast Thou stayed us when we falter.
Here dost Thou to our prayer attend.
When weary, weak and heavy laden,
Within this place we sought Thy peace.
To youth and age, to man and maiden,
Have come the joy that shalt not cease.
Here have we seen Thy face.

Here have we heard Thy voice,
　　Comrade and Guide.
Beneath this roof we have been near Thee.
Within these walls we feel and hear Thee.
Here press Thy hand and touch Thy side.
'Neath loftier arches be Thou with us still,
Our friend, our comrade, and our cheer.
Thy presence ampler spaces fill,
And make Thy dwelling there as here.
There may we hear Thy voice.

IN PROFUNDIS

Why must the old men die,
Clutching at life, while I
Longing to let it slip,
Find the bitter cup still at my lip?

To them, each moment, emptied of delight,
Is precious still in their enfeebled sight.
Age has brought every wisdom but the lore
Gladly to lose what they can keep no more.

BY THY LOVE UNDYING

(Sung to Greig's *Stella Maris*)

By thy love undying,
On thy grace relying,
    We thy faulty children seek thy face and favor.
By thy courage ever
Aid our weak endeavor.
    Strengthen thou our spirits not to faint or waver.

With thy patience endless,
Friend of all though friendless,
    Teach us from thy wisdom, meek yet ever glorious.
Gentle, wise and daring,
Forward ever faring,
    Lead us till we triumph, o'er the world victorious.

FOR AN HOUR

I may not keep the heights I gain
    In those rare hours of ecstasy
When, scorning ease, despising pain,
    Forgetting self, and winning free
    From all that most entangles me,
I leave the low miasmic plain
    Of sloth and doubt and greed, to be
Companion of the heavenly train
Who tread the loftier ways; who keep
    A tryst with stars, nor shrink nor cower
In craven fear or sluggish sleep,
    Nor seek the ease of blossomed bower.
    My earthbound soul lacks breath and power
To hold a path so nobly steep.
    Yet God be praised that for an hour
I gained the heights I could not keep.

EASTER MORNING

Gray clouds against a leaden sky,
  Unlit by any glow of dawn.
Two weeping women hasten by
  Whose love still lives though hope is gone.

The day breaks dull and red, without
  A cheering ray for those who grieve.
Two men come running who dare not doubt
  The thing they dare not yet believe.

The tomb is open. He lives! He lives!
  Shout with one exultant voice.
The night is gone. The fair sun gives
  His gift of gold. Rejoice! Rejoice!

Again the darkness closes in
  Upon a world grown cold and wise—
The gloom of greed, the murk of sin—
  When men forget his shining eyes.

Roll back the clouds of hate, and fling
  Apart the curtains of the night.
In hearts that love and souls that sing,
  Let Christ arise. Let there be light!

TEMPTATION

They took him to a mountaintop to see
Where earth's fair kingdoms flung their golden net
To snare the feet and trick the souls of men.
With slimy craft and cynic guile they said:
If he but sees the glory and the pride,
The pomps and pleasure of this tinsel world,
He will forget his splendid futile dreams.
And so they took him up and tempted him.

They pointed far across their level earth,
East to the fabled empires of the Ind,
Whose rulers' power was as the power of gods,
Where caravans with tinkling camel bells
Brought silks and perfumes, pearls and ivory,
And tribute from far humbled provinces;
South to the magic kingdom of the Nile,
To Nubia and Abyssinia,
Jungle and desert kingdoms, rude but rich
With slaves and gems and golden yellow sands;
Northward to barbarous lands but dimly seen,
Savage but surging with unmeasured strength;
West where Rome's empire sent her legions forth,
Conquering, building, ruling with wise force,
The mighty mother of an unborn brood
Of nations which should rise and rule the world.

All this they spread before him, tempting him,
And watched to see ambition light his eye,
The lust of power darken his bright face,
And avarice crook his hands to clutch the gold.

But from the mountain peak he raised his eyes,
And saw the deep, calm sky, the stars, and God.

CONFESSIO FIDEO

I have no care for what the world may do to me,
For I have riches that it cannot take
And poverty that it cannot enrich—
And the rest does not greatly matter.
I love life, but I do not fear death,
For it is cool and comforting and friendly.
I enjoy ease and splendid idleness,
But I can sleep soundly on a hard bed,
And hurry without being rushed,
And work to weariness yet not be fretted.

Even pain is oftener friend than enemy,
And the fear of it is more poignant than the pain of it.
I am not apprehensive about the loss of friends,
For they cannot be lost while we are worthy of each other.

It is good to have things beautiful about one—
Pictures and books, a garden and a house;
And a good fiddle is a great help, too—
But it is not bad to be without them,
To tread the path without baggage,
To have only what all men have, or could if they would;
For the colors of the dawn are cheap and stars cost nothing.
If the hands are empty, they may all the better
Fling greetings to the world, embrace dear friends,
Or be uplifted in oblations of pure gratitude.
It is not bitter to be scorned for empty-handedness
When one has learned to pity all the scorners.

I am not indifferent to the things men buy with money,
And I will work as hard as any man ought to get them,
But I refuse to get excited about them,
Or to bow down and worship them,
Or to think of them as necessary,
Or to lose a friend to win a kingdom,
Or to uproot one flower of fancy
To lay the foundation of a marble palace.
I will work today for a guerdon long deferred;
I will labor to plant a tree in the distant hope of fruit—
Perhaps not for my gathering and eating—
For ease is not important,
And planting is as beautiful as harvesting.
But I will not poison a moment with fear or anger,
Or starve a day with empty-heartedness.
Who kills a day of fragrant loveliness
Kills an inch of himself: for life is a day, and a day, and a
        day.

There are many waters in the sea:
The surface is whipped to foam,
Thundering waves roll over it,
Dangerous gales sweep it,
And every little boat is tossed and driven;
And men say: 'The sea is rough.'
But the real sea is very calm.
Only on the surface are the threatening surges men think
    dangerous.

They are dangerous—to those who live on the surface.
But there are no dangers in the quiet depths.
All the billows have gone over me—
But it is a small matter, for the billows are not the ocean.
My dwelling is not in the waves of circumstance,
But deep in the peaceful, infinite ocean of life.

The sky is high past all imagining.
A child can touch the place where it begins,
But sight, imagination, and mathematics placed end to end
Can never reach the top.
At the bottom, in a thin stratum of variable weather,
Clouds, winds, and lightnings threaten, bluster, flash—
And men say: "The sky is stormy."
But the deep sky, the real sky, is never stormy.
My sky is not this negligible sediment of clouds,
This film of murk,
This agitated curtain of unrest
Draping the door that leads to illimitable quiet.
My sky is the vast where stars move silently
In the peace of the presence of God.

Therefore I shall not be troubled by what the world may
    do to me
Because it can do nothing that matters.

VIA CRUCIS

A pilgrim plods a lonely road
    Toward a goal but dimly seen.
His back is bowed beneath a load,
    But his eyes are kind and keen.
The beckoning light, so faint, so far—
Is it a candle-lit window, a star,
Or the court of heaven where angels are
    Behind a glittering screen?

The pilgrim nears the glistening height,
    The end of his wise desire,
A lofty goal, so dazzling bright
    He could not but aspire.
His eager eyes he turns to it;
His heart wth longing yearns to it;
The flame within him burns to it
    Like an altar's holy fire.

Through towns and streets with a friendly nod,
    Through fields with a winsome smile,
He had followed the trail to the mountain of God
    Many a hopeful mile.
Then up rose a cross in the way to it.
Ah, what shall the pilgrim say to it—
A Yea, or a trembling Nay to it
    And its menace harsh and vile?

The price of the end is the long, long way.
    The price of gain is loss.
Who seeks pure gold must burn away
    The alloy and the dross.
He may go to the left or right of it,
Or turn him back at the sight of it,
Or faint in horror or fright of it—
    But the cost of a goal is a cross.

PILOTS ARE WE

(a response to "No Pilots We," by John Jay Chapman)

The winds of fortune and of circumstance
Beat on our fragile bark of destiny,
And every shifting gust and fickle chance
Of storm or calm seems mightier than we.
The tides move rhythmic'ly, resistlessly.
Stars in their courses, careless of our fret,
Rise as God calls them from the orient sea,
Move as He bids, and, as He bids them, set.
Wind, tide, and stars ask not our puny aid; and yet—

Pilots are we; and the divine commands
Come from the deep mysterious heart of things,
Not to the ship, but to the man who stands
Grasping the helm with brave though trembling hands,
Steers by a star, and, as he labors, sings.
We needs must trust the billowed sea that rings
Us round with mysteries till the senses reel;
Listen to every whispering voice that brings
Divine commands, each cosmic impulse feel,
Accept the tides and stars—yet labor at the wheel.

THE UNFINISHED SYMPHONY

A spinning clot of ooze and slime,
   With a core of fire and a shroud of murk,
Whirled through the void in the dawn of time
   When the Lord had finished his first day's work.

Two spirits lean over the rail and peer
   At the ugly, lifeless thing. Said one:
"I never saw such a ghastly sphere.
   This is the worst that the Lord has done.

"A clod of mud and a flicker of fire,
   So unlike heaven, and yet so near it—
From that foul mass of steaming mire
   Never can come a living spirit."

The other said: "I think not so.
   Far down the future I seem to see
Living creatures that come and go
   With a will of their own. And whether it be

"That the Lord will do some strange new deed
   In kindling them by his inbreathed breath,
Or whether it happens that the seed
   Of life lies hid in this stuff of death,

"I cannot tell. But a race of men
   Will arise and seek, though their light be dim,
For beauty and truth and love, and then
   They shall rejoice like the seraphim."

But the first one laughed as again he spoke
   And downed the prophecy with a thud:
"There is nothing in fire but ashes and smoke,
   And only dust can come from mud."

✶ ✶ ✶

Who knows that human heart and nerve—
   Life as we live it and death as we fear it—
Are the topmost reach of the soaring curve
   That started in mire and climbed to spirit?

If hope and love grew out of the flesh,
   As flesh grew out of the steaming clod,
Shall life not slip through the prisoning mesh
   To loftier levels still untrod?

THE QUEST

I sought for God in field and hill,
   In lonely paths, in crowded ways.
I sought Him when my heart was still
   In words of prayer and hymns of praise.
In mystic mood and subtle thought
   I sought Him, but I found Him not.

I fled from God with craven fear
   To hide from Him my nakedness.
The words I spoke He must not hear;
   The thoughts I nursed He must not guess.
Oh to be hidden and forgot!
   I fled, but I escaped Him not.

I found a friend who trusted me,
   Yet knew my weakness through and through.
I found a task that seemed to be
   Too bitter hard, yet mine to do.
In love and work I found my soul,
Forgot my quest—but reached my goal.

Fantasies and Diversions

THE SWIMMER

He floats between two blues
    In a world all motion and light,
Where earth and heaven fuse
    And the waves of both unite
      In one encompassing surge of liquid depth and height.

Hot passion's flaming red,
    And hatred's scorching hues,
And the black of the sad and the dead
    Fade into naught, and lose
      Their heat and hate and pain in comforting, healing
        blues.

In an ocean of sky and wave,
    And a heaven of wave and sky—
All one—blue billows lave
    The soul which, released, can fly
      In the four-dimensional space that all souls crave.

A world all plastic and free,
    Where fixed things disappear,
Where the changeless ceases to be
In the flow of the sky and the sea—
    All things are possible here.
      And the gulls swoop past and soar, and the swallows
        flit and peer.

THE WANDERER

Dusk on a prairie farm, a thousand miles from the sea.
 The cows are in and the chores are done.
 The stars are coming one by one,
And a prisoned soul is free.
The farmhouse fades like a fairy thing, and a fettered soul
 goes free.

There's an offshore wind tonight. The tide will turn at
 ten.
 The scudding moon is cutting its way
 Through billows of cloud. We only stay
For the tide, my merry men.
So man the capstan. Yo, heave ho! Heave ho! my bully
 men.

We have filled the hold with copra. We have piled the
 deck with bales
 Of silks from every road that ran
 From Tokio to Ispahan,
From Malabar to Wales.
 The riches of the Orient lie beneath our purple sails.

There's ivory and incense. There's indigo and tea.
 There's sandalwood from Mandalay,
 And pearls like eggs from Arabay,
And Persian tapestry,
And we've treasures in the cabin men would give their
 eyes to see.

Oh, bravely have we voyaged through tempest and
 typhoon,
 By Polynesian coral isles.
 Through jungle rivers, miles on miles,
Beneath the tropic moon.
We're homeward bound, but we shall make another
 voyage soon.

For we have found an island southeast of Ararat
  Where Turkish pirates hid their gold,
  And all the treasure caves of old
Are naught compared with that—
"Yes, Ma. I've wound the clock and I'll put out the cat."

GOING-TO-THE-SUN

(in Glacier Park)

Going-to-the-Sun Mountain lifts its head
Four thousand feet above St. Mary's Lake
In a circle of stalwart mountains pressing close—
Red Eagle, Little Chief, Citadel, Fusilade, Goat—
Shouldering each other roughly for place at the front,
Tiptoeing, craning their necks, peering to see
What wonder lies in the blue depth of St. Mary's.
They have looked long but have not yet seen it all.
Eager, expectant after a million years
Of gazing, still they gaze, seeing a little
Every day, and waiting some greater glory.

They are surely there, for I saw them yesterday.
It took them aeons to grow to such a height
And get their front-row places at the scene—
A scene which they themselves both make and witness.
They will not leave overnight. But now, invisible,
Unseeing and unseen, they wait in patience.
I cannot see them; they cannot see the lake.
It is no day for eyes. The blind could see
As far as any in this veiling fog.
What matter? If I see only what I see now,
Then am I blind and dull and miserable.
Yesterday's sight is this day's happy vision.

Then hail, Sun Mountain, behind your curtaining cloud,
Hidden and revealed as by a silver tissue,
Like all persistent blessed memories.

ROADS

Give me a trail on the mountainside
    Where the spruce and the aspen grow,
With a single comrade staunch and tried,
    And the world spread out below.
I look aloft to the glistening peak;
    I press the flower-gemmed sod;
And I hear the voice of the mountain speak
    Of beauty, and strength, and God.

Give me a road through the countryside
    Where the fields are broad and fair,
And the maples fling their branches wide,
    For the homes of men are there.
It may be far from city and town,
    Or it may be little worth,
But every road leads up and down
    To the farthest ends of earth.

Nay, give me a street on the old West Side,
    Where the throngs of people are;
Where beat the waves of the human tide
    To the din of wagon and car.
In shops and flats and shining lights
    I find my soul again;
For what is a world of wondrous sights
    Apart from the world of men?

LIGHTNING

Beneath the lightning's vicious stab, which seems
    The gesture of omnipotence gone mad,
I meekly bow, confessing in its gleams
    Such power as men or angels never had.
So unimportant and so frail am I,
    So impotent to stay its threatened ill—
Yet more than match for any angry sky,
    For I can say: I love; I ought; I will.

DAILY BREAD

Oh, I am rich in treasures stored away—
Old ecstasies and half-remembered joys;
Prismatic dawns that faded to white noons;
Knowledge forgotten; songs my mother sang;
The scent of flowers that withered long ago;
Wounds that have healed and left but little scars
To show where once the very lifeblood ebbed;
Sorrows that long since lost their bitterness
And only knit me closer to my kind;
Music that lingers though its notes are stilled;
Voices and hands and lips that I have loved.
These are my wealth, my comfort, and my stay.
But not on these my soul can feed today.

Holding in dear remembrance all that was,
Guarding my treasures with a miser's care,
May I have yet some daily meed of joy:
Some fresh, untasted cup; some flower that springs
From the deep soil of old experience
But blossoms in the sunlight of this hour.
Rather some sorrow, fresh and fierce and keen,
Than the stale dregs and ashes of old joys
Too dearly cherished. Grant me, Lord, new songs,
New lifting of the heart with each new morn.
Give me this day my spirit's daily bread.

MANY MOONS, I

Alien and cold, white as the face of the dead,
Why do you gaze with that fixed, contemptuous stare?
Harsh critic of all human warmth and frailty;
All eyes, no heart; all keen, unfeeling vision,
No kindly understanding of men's ways;
You watch the generations come and go,
Yourself unchanging; only a deep, slow breathing,

A monthly alternation of staring insolence
And a thin, wry, bitter smile of deep contempt.
Oh ghastly face, inhuman luminary!
Beauty and love to us are new and wonderful;
To you, stale, vapid, commonplace, and gross.
You hate all youth and scorn its fine fresh ardor
With cynic bitterness and lofty laughter.
You would be wise—if you had not forgotten
What every simple youth and maiden knows.

MANY MOONS, II

Now comes the friendly spirit of the night,
A presence potent but impalpable,
Tiptoeing down the path her own beams make,
Entering through six little window panes,
Stretching at ease upon the counterpane,
Kissing the pillow, and spreading her bright hair over it,
Elfin as starlight, warm as wood firelight,
Coming from far but confidently at home,
Comradely, comforting, gracious, yet mysterious.
Saint Anthony might receive her uncorrupted
And in good conscience, but not all unmoved.
In such celestial company I live
Not in one world, but two. For down and up
That silver ladder, as in Jacob's dream,
Troop spirits that bring harmony and peace,
And there is traffic between earth and heaven.

MANY MOONS, III

Aloof and exquisite, danseuse of the night,
Hidden and veiled except for one arched eyebrow,
What dithyrambic dance, O chaste bacchante,
Tilts your one visible eye to such a slant?
How must the heavens reel with that wild maze,
Circling, swirling, gyrating, pirouetting!

"*Ex pede, Herculem!*" And from the curve
Of that one telltale eyebrow may be known
The unrestraint of your heaven-circling dance.
Praise be to earth—so solid, steady moving,
Placid and practical and right-side-up—
For a fixed footing in the cosmic swirl.
Yet praise to you, lithe lady of the moon,
Divinely irresponsible, irrepressibly buoyant,
Giving to us, earthbound in level places,
Veiled glimpse of revelries beyond our reach.

"*MARCH!*"

"March!" is the crisp and curt command
   The calendar gives to the armies of spring,
In the training camps in the far southland
   Where they have been drilling and marshaling—
   Birds all poised on eager wing,
Warm winds drenched with rain and sun,
   And every leafy and twining thing
Ready to start and move as one.

   And the buds of the lilac under the bark
   Wait for the signal there in the dark.

The robin scout goes far ahead
   To spy out the enemy's land and sing
A note of defiance. The osiers' red
   Is a flag of revolt in the name of spring.
   But discipline fails as the armies fling
Into action with joy in the glorious fray,
   And soon they are dancing and rioting
In the wild abandon of April and May.

   For ever-invading spring's advance
   Begins in March but ends in a dance.

MUSIC

Music of waves, murmur of bees,
Rustling of wind in the sycamore trees,
  Thrush note, dove note,
  Meadowlark's love note,
Nightingale's love song under the moon,
  Sibilant sounds of the whispering breeze,
Soft breathing of earth in the hushed summer noon,
  Voices of twilight when day's at an end—
But clearer and dearer and sweeter than these
Is the best of all music,
  The voice of a friend.

SPRING'S CONSPIRACY

I sense a desperate conspiracy
  Of all the myriad dull, insensate things
That leap to life with vernal ecstasy,
  Of everything with feathers, fur, or wings,

Of wind, and all the odors that it brings,
  Of shifting lights and colors on the sea,
Of all that flutters, whispers, hums, or sings,
  Or makes mute music and dumb melody.

They plot against efficiency and work,
  Against the peace and dignity of all
Who walk on pavements, live in flats, and lurk
  In offices or shops or learning's hall.

The potent combination of these foes,
  These crafty enemies of industry,
And all their machinations are, God knows,
  More than a match for mortal frailty.

So, since I know not aught that I can do
  To circumvent their wiles, my only chance
Is to join fortune with the blessed crew
  As one of spring's conspiring miscreants.

VILLANELLE

Rede me the riddle of that ancient rune;
It might have meaning yet for such as us:
Night comes too late and morning comes too soon.

When has an angel spread his wings at noon
To make the garish day more glorious?
Rede me the riddle of that ancient rune.

Work is medicinal and toil a boon
If pain and passion are contiguous.
Night comes too late and morning comes too soon.

The soaring plane or sky-borne slow balloon
May make the sunrise seem fortuitous.
Rede me the riddle of that ancient rune.

Earthbound below, pedestrian platoon,
We plod the path fate has assigned to us.
Night comes too late and morning comes too soon.

At last the fading day unveils the moon.
There are some things one cannot well discuss.
Rede me the riddle of that ancient rune:
Night comes too late and morning comes too soon.

A BOOK

Softly I closed the book, as in a dream,
And let its echoes linger to redeem
Silence with music, darkness with its gleam.

That day I worked no more. I could not bring
My hands to toil, my thoughts to trafficking.
A new light shone on every common thing.

Celestial splendors flamed before my gaze.
That day I worked no more; but, to God's praise,
I shall work better all my other days.

STARS, I

If they would only let us see the stars
As friendly twinkling eyes in heaven's face,
Kindly and intimate, not very large
Nor in such unimaginable space;
Or as the glistening diamond dust of dew
Upon the pleasant meadows of the sky;
Or as the silver lace upon the gowns
Of gentle maids who smilingly pass by;

Or as the notes of music written o'er
An ample staff where all may see and sing
Like choristers who read a common score—
They would seem very close and comforting.
But when with labored art some meddling sage
Reckons the orbit of each separate star,
Tells of light-years, and calculates their age,
They are too old, too monstrous, and too far.

Stunned with immensity and drunk with space,
Bewildered pilgrim in a world too wide,
I seek the shelter of some narrow place
Where things of frail and timid beauty hide:
A rocky tidal pool wherein a hand
Ruthlessly dipped would be a blow of fate;
The print of wind-waved grass tips on the sand
A careless gesture might obliterate.

How shall I live with all these million suns
Circling the universe in fiery rings,
I who am content to contemplate
The quiet beauty of the smallest things?
For I can never feel myself at home
Beneath a roof a billion miles above,
Or wholly happy underneath a dome
So much too vast for humble hearts to love.

STARS, II

It was a passing timid mood—that thought
About the terror of too vast a sky;
A momentary cowardice that fought
Against a sense of space too wide and high;
Perhaps a strange inverted vertigo
Which, looking up, felt dizziness and fear;
Perhaps a clinging to the things below,
So small, so safe, so infinitely dear.

There is a matchless and a boundless charm
In beauties closer than the distant skies—
The world that can be circled with an arm,
Infinities condensed within two eyes,
The shelter of a low room, candle-lit,
Felicity all focussed in one spot.
What far-flung splendors can compare with it,
What grandeur satisfy if this does not?

But life is made of mingled great and small,
Conflicting urges, strange antinomies;
Of following duty's low insistent call,
And seeking freedom under spacious skies,
Of looking in and down to precious things
In precious places guarded by love's bars,
And looking out and up with wonderings
And yearnings to the mountains and the stars.

So, to the tiny quiet pool the surge
Of rising tides shall bring a deeper peace.
Let waves pour into it again and merge
Its quietness with all the untamed seas.
And if the house be narrow, let it be
One that looks out on mountains yet untrod.
Let there be windows opening on the sea.
Let there be stars above. Let there be God.

BIG THINGS

How big a thing have you ever seen?
Bigger than large is what I mean—
Stupendous—a thing that batters your eyes
With sheer, unspeakable, measureless size,
And then, while all your senses ache
With the wounds its mass and hugeness make,
Pours upon them a strange high peace
And the balm of beauty to give surcease
To the blissful agony of being
Gripped by the things too great for seeing.
Lovely to look at, easy to grasp.
You don't get that from little things,
No flower that blows, no bird that sings
Can make a human stagger and gasp
With the pain of growing large enough
To stand in the presence of primitive stuff
Molded and made on a cosmic plan
To humble, exalt, and intoxicate man.

What have you seen that is big like that
Among the things you have ever looked at?
Stars don't count, and you know why.
The chances are you have never seen them
Except as pinholes in the sky
With a little stretch of dark between them.
The sea, if it's rough, you may put in your credit,
Especially if it is all around you
Heaving and towering—love it or dread it—
Trying its deadly worst to drown you.
And the desert—well, you're not to blame
For doubting it has a friendly soul
If ever you've had your horse go lame
Forty miles from a water hole.
But hate it or love it—it's much the same—
Once you are caught in that golden bowl
Ringed with the distant mountain rim

Misty purple and spirit-dim,
You will know the world is not so small.
You will know what distance means—that's all.
And you will find—whatever you bring;
Nothing much, and everything.

God knew his job when he made the stars—
You can count them in if you learn to see—
Let us see great things through the prisoning bars
And put in our hearts eternity.
The small things have their use, no doubt—
Jewel and dewdrop, fern and flower—
But the cramped and shriveled eyes cry out
For the sight of space and the sense of power.

OUTSIDE THE DOOR

There was a feast, a glorious feast,
  With wine and wit and laughter.
The tides of joy ran full, nor ceased
Till dawn was glowing in the east
  And day came following after.
And even then the rout increased
  And rang from roof and rafter.
    All hearts were tuned to sweet accord,
    For mirth was king and love was lord.

Another feast, another night,
  With joy and jest and singing,
With foods as rich, and flowers as bright.
With wines as rare and hearts as light,
  And laughter loudly ringing.
And yet a shadow dimmed the sight,
  A tinge of sadness bringing.
    More pain than joy to me it bore,
    For I—I was outside the door.

TWO HOUSES

I have a house by the side of the road
    And a house in the heart of the dunes,
In one I carry the daily load,
    In the other I make my tunes.

It is better to live in the busy town
    Than to dwell in the woods alone,
For even the din of its mirth and sin
    Has a music of its own,

And people are better than empty space,
    And streets more friendly than sod,
And more than the sky does a human face
    Reflect the smile of God.

But the grip of the city is rough and strong
    And its burdens bear me down.
So I go to the country to find a song—
    And bring it back to town.

THE REPENTANT THIEF

Time gave, and time has taken away.
    So sighs the race of saddened men.
The rose that blossomed yesterday
    Tomorrow dies, nor lives again.

The joys that are but memories,
    The sweet experience too soon past,
The scenes and sounds we loved—all these
    Were far too delicate to last.

But while the heart with anguish burns
    For loss of all we could not fetter,
Time—the repentant thief—returns
    With something better.

THE TROUBADOUR

(Just off the *Rue des Ecoles,* in Paris, stands a
bronze troubadour, lute dropped, hand on hilt,
interrupted and alert. In the moments before and
after the interruption, he may have said something
like this.)

Drop me the crimson rose in your hair,
    Star of my darkness—nay, dawn to my night.
    Shine in my gloom with your perfect light,
Lady aloft in your balcony there.
Drop me the rose that you deign to wear,
    Doubling its beauty and shaming its grace.
    Give me a glimpse of your matchless face
And toss me the red rose from your hair.

But soft! I hear the tread of feet
    And the tinkle of music drawing near.
    Whose is the hateful voice I hear,
And whose is the form at the bend of the street?
Back, draw back, oh lady sweet,
    Into the shadow. Lie there, my lute.
    Only a moment your strings shall be mute
While, dagger in hand, this churl I meet.

. . . .

Pardon the interlude, lady fair.
    My crimsoned blade again is bright.
    The moon is softer, and sweeter the night
Since his breath no longer pollutes the air.
So give me a glance and a glimpse, oh rare
    And lovely lady. Your troubadour
    Awaits the smile of his *reine d'amour,*
Begging the red rose from your hair.

42

A SNOW-FLOWER

(A surprise meeting with my daughter on a rough winter day)

A sudden vision of grace
   In a world of ice and snow!
Like a shaft of light in a murky place,
Like a glow of warmth in frozen space
   (How marvelous its glow!),
Like a single rose in an earthen vase,
Was that vibrant form and radiant face.
   From what soil can such flowers grow?

The earth must be friendly within,
   For all its hostile show.
It must be calm beneath its din,
Bright and joyous and sound and clean
   (How bright we cannot know),
Pure below its visible sin,
Deep down where the roots of things begin,
   And warm beneath its snow.

TO MURIEL AT 12

Make good, sweet maid.
Be good, and also clever.
Let heart and soul maturing
Match the growth
Of disciplined intelligence.
And never
Let any tell you
That you can't be both.

ADVENTURE

Over the next near hilltop
   Or through the garden gates,
Or just around the turn of the road
   The great adventure waits.

But when I top the summit,
　　No marvels greet my eyes;
Only a sunlit plain in which
　　No fairy cities rise.

The gates of the wonderful garden
　　Swing open to my hand,
But within are only common flowers
　　And weeds and dirt and sand.

The winding trail allures
　　With a promise of glad surprise,
But it straightens into a dull highway
　　That mocks my eager eyes.

But beyond the plain is a hilltop;
　　Beyond the garden, a gate.
There is always another turn of the road
　　Where the great adventures wait.

And when my ears heed not,
　　And when my heart is cold
To the call of the road and the gate and the hill,
　　I shall know that I am old.

AN OLD MAN
(to J. H. G., 1929)

I know a man, an old man, who keeps a heart of youth,
Who learns a little every day and stays abreast with truth,
Who loves to think of his boyhood, so very long ago,
But loves still more to watch the boys today and see them
　　　　grow;
To see them learn the things that he has known for many
　　　　years,
And if they learn some new things he is glad and never
　　　　fears.
He never fears that wisdom will be dead when he is gone,

For he knows it grows from age to age as the world goes
   moving on.
And so he never lets his faith in God and man grow dim,
And it isn't strange that young men also keep their faith
   in him.
He keeps his troubles to himself and spreads his joys afar.
He feeds his soul on friendship and on mountain, sea,
   and star.
His face is bright with sunset light, but he greets the
   coming dawn
With such a buoyant hope that all the dread of night is
   gone.
Such wonderful preservatives are Beauty, Good, and
   Truth.
God bless the man, the old man, who keeps a heart of
   youth.

SOUTHBOUND

Surely there was magic in the air last night,
For I went to sleep in April and came awake in May.
If the moon wove misty magic over everything in sight,
It was quite to be expected after such a magic day.
The last I saw of April was a fleet of leafless trees
Scudding north at midnight like ships without a sail,
Bare masts bending, rigging taut and trembling,
Racing north by moonlight as though driven by a gale.
I couldn't quite see it, but I knew there was a lake
Just beyond the trees and the gaunt steel mills.
And the time was early April, there could be no mistake,
For not the sheerest gauze of green was spread upon the
   hills.
It may have been the moon that came and kissed me on
   the mouth
While the bare trees scudded northward—or was I
   scudding south?

Then the sun came, sudden as the red gods come,
And dogwood, redbud, apple-blossom, plum
Were dancing past the window in a morris maze
With their green gowns flying in a gold-green haze.
Instead of the lake came a bank-full river;
I counted ninety seconds while it slid below;
And lazy blue smoke was curling up from a shantyboat
Moored in a bayou and ready to go.

It was reasonable magic wrought by such a night and day
That I went to sleep in April and woke to find it May.

AT CARCASSONNE

Down the valleys of Languedoc,
Where ghosts of knights and troubadours flock,
Hiding by day and riding by night
When the moonlit road is silvery white—
So we journeyed on and on
Up to the City of Carcassonne.
Three score towers against the sky,
Like mailed fists clenched and lifted high,
Tall battlements, a grim chateau,
And round and round the gray walls go.
A drawbridge here, a postern there,
Loopholes for archers everywhere;
And moat and scarpe and barbicans,
All built in the days of high romance.
Gaul and Roman, Goth and Moor
Fought and wrought on this hill, and sure
If ever war was glorified
By chivalry and song beside,
It must have been when Charles the Great,
Simon de Montfort or Louis the Saint
Stormed this town or held its towers,
And tournaments filled the quieter hours;
Or when Bernart Alanhan of old Narbonne,
As a troubadour guest at Carcassonne,

Sang of the brave knights' feats of war
And the beautiful ladies they did them for.
Troubadours, ladies, and knights are gone.
No flags fly over Carcassonne
Save the banners of sunset aflame in the sky
As the one-armed watchman passes by.
Here in the scenes of old Romance,
He lifts a voice for peace in France.
He told me his story yesterday,
And now he halts on his round to say:
"How noble this business of fighting appears
Through the mist and haze of a thousand years.
Still they call it 'right against wrong,'
And deck it with banners and bugles and song;
But this I pray God and Our Lady for:
In my children's time, may there be no war."

VENITE, AMICI

A school song for the Claremont School for Boys,
1913-1921
(to the tune of Adeste Fideles)

Venite, amici ac sodales cari,
Cantate cum gaudio ex corde pleno.
Venite, cantate, libenter jubilate
   Laudate scholam nostram,
   Magistros et matronam,
   Laudate Clarum Montem
    Cum gaudio.

Mox discedemus a nostra alma matre,
Mox committemus nos mari vitae.
Ave et vale, care Mons Praeclare.
   To nos omnes laudamus;
   Te filii amamus;
   Te semper salutamus
    Ad saecula.

NIGHT ON THE DESERT

The Desert sleeps. Vast, silent, and serene,
She puts aside the glittering cloth-of-gold
In which the day had mantled her, and cold
And somber lies, untroubled and unseen.
She sleeps—but dreams again on those old days
When conquerers came to plant the flag of Spain,
Noble and knight rode proudly o'er her plain.
Unmoved she bides, while they have gone their ways.

Changeless beneath the stars she bares her breast
And mirrors back their mystery and calm,
Earth's treasure-house of patience, silence, rest,
Richer than all the lands of vine and palm.
No turmoil here. Here fevered struggles cease.
And in her dream she whispers, *Here is peace.*

THE COWARD

He hid his pain beneath a smile,
 Courageous as a stoic.
He bore his burden many a mile
 With fortitude heroic.

Fate was unkind. Love passed him by.
 He learned to do without it.
Then, proud of his modest bravery,
 The coward told about it.

Christmas Messages

MERRY IS FOR CHRISTMAS

MERRY is for *Christmas*.
From reverent joy and prayerful gratitude
Let your rejoicing for this day and season
Rise to the highest pitch of jubilation.
Let laughter ring and no harsh note be sounded.
This is a time for giving and forgiving.
Forget the bonds of coldness and of caution
That cramp our hearts and chill our human warmth.
Let mirth abound and high hilarity,
While Love reigns over all.

HAPPY is for the whole *New Year*.
It cannot be continuous ecstasy,
Unbroken sunshine or perpetual June.
You would not want a year of merriment.
But may it be a year of happiness,
With work and play, with toil and rest, in balance,
With rhythm of gravity and gaiety,
And through it all deep, lasting satisfaction
In both the doing and the work that's done.
It can be so, if Love reigns over all.

A B C D E F G H I J K L M
N O P Q R S T U V W X Y Z

Behold, dear Friend, the Alphabet.
Its six-and-twenty letters, set
In order due and right array,
Say all the things that man can say.
They voice all passions, state all truth,
Express the heart of age and youth.
They hold philosophy, and wit,
And song, and mirth, and every bit
Of poetry and eloquence,
Of lofty thought and homely sense,
And every joyous, friendly thing
That men can write or say or sing.
Here are the rugged words of friends
Who clasp hands where the journey ends,
And tender messages of cheer
To those far off yet closely dear.
And so, instead of sending you
Merely a Christmas wish or two,
With lordly generosity
(Which still does not impoverish me)
I give you the whole mine from which
Are dug those treasures rare and rich,
The raw material for each word
By which the hearts of men are stirred.

Take this crude stuff of poetry
And, with your better wit, be free
To find in it—as you can do—
The things that I would say to you.
These unset jewels—make of them
A necklace, chain, or diadem;
And read, with friendship's second sight,
The words I dare not try to write.

We gave you once the *alphabet* complete.
　The stuff from which is fashioned every word
Of hope and joy and love with which men greet
　　Their friends, and all the poems ever heard,
　　The records of all things that have occurred,
The messages of prophets, seers, and sages
And all the wit and wisdom of the ages.

Now with these *notes* make symphony and song.
　These are the wondrous twelve. There are no more
Weave them in patterns, make them short or long,
　　Blend them with skill, and you will have the score
　　Of melodies and harmonies galore,
For all the music ever sung or played
From just these simple elements is made.

So, as our Christmas greeting to you, friend,
　Accept the music that can come to birth
Out of these magic notes we gladly send.
　　Meagre their cost but infinite their worth,
　　For they can scatter joy through all the earth.
With *words* of wisdom and with *notes* of praise,
May you have harmony through all your days.

WINTER WARMTH

If, in some month not sacred to good will
As this one is, or in some time of stress,
The tedious dull details of living press
Upon you till the world seems deadly ill;

If, in bright June perhaps or August's heat,
You find your heart is not so warm as now,
And you are chill and lone, you know not how,
Amid the strident voices of the street—

51

Remember then the gladness of these days.
Their human warmth and love divine remember.
Quicken to flame the faintly glowing ember
Of faith and cheer. Seek for the friendly ways.
And let the Yuletide radiance of December
Brighten and warm your Aprils and your Mays.

THEY MIGHT HAVE SAID

Milton might have said:

Sing, Sacred Muse, and strike the sounding lyre.
    Let earth rejoice and heaven with anthems ring.
Hark to the music of the angelic choir
    That hails the Son of heaven's eternal King.

John Donne might have said:

Catch the swiftly falling star
    That came to mark the Savior's birth.
It shall rise and gleam afar
    To light all time and all the earth.

Wordsworth might have said:

My heart leaps up when I recall
    That wondrous radiant morn
    When Christ was born,
A day of joy for men and angels all.
Dark was the waiting world without him.
    But trailing clouds of glory did he come
    Down from his heavenly home.
Earth's prison shades could never close about him.

Shelley might have said:

O wild west wind, hush thy ambiguous voice
    This sacred morn. Then trumpet to the earth
The note of prophecy. Let men rejoice
    That, winter past, spring blossoms with his birth.

BETWEEN THE LINES

The season bids us now again,
> *The wise men saw at Bethlehem*
In common with all honest men,
> *The star that long had guided them,*
To hail the happy time and say,
> *And wise men now, where'er they are,*
Be merry on this Christmas Day.
> *Will still be guided by that star.*

With smiles and gifts we greet each friend.
> *The laughter of this festal time*
Laughter and song their echoes blend.
> *The glitter, the sweet jangling chime,*
Candles and holly and mistletoe
> *Are good, but underneath them lies*
Make bright the scene. Heigh-ho, heigh-ho!
> *A deeper sense, the glad surprise*

The holly, bells, and vague goodwill
> *Of finding in the gift divine*
To all mankind are lovely; still
> *A human quality so fine*
More meaning lies within these signs,
> *Of love and peace that men can still*
So let us read between the lines.
> *Live as brothers, if they will.*

CHRISTMAS EVE IN BILLINGS HOSPITAL

The doctor knows best,
But it does seem a pity.
He says I must rest
While all over the city
Christmas is near
With its mirth and its cheer.

As a hospital guest
I will welcome it here
With this jubilant ditty,
For this much is clear—
Christmas can't be repressed.
It will seem rather queer
But it must be confessed
That the doctor knows best—
Yet it *does* seem a pity.

✦ ✦ ✦

Wherever a window opens wide
And a strip of the sky shows blue
Wherever the heart is satisfied
And wishes are coming true,
Wherever comes the thought of a friend
Or the light of a wished-for face,
There the joys of Christmas lend
Their blessings to the place.

(So the doctor sent me home at 8 P.M., after the University Glee Club had sung carols at the door of my hospital room.)

AT THE GATE

(On the cover of *The Christian-Evangelist,* January 1, 1903)

Lift up your heads; unfold, ye doors;
    Be lifted up, ye gates!
Before the New Year's portal now
    The King of Glory waits.
The gray dawn breaks; the new day wakes;
    The bells of New Year ring.
Throw wide the gateway of the year
    And welcome in the King.

The hosts of Pride and Greed and Hate,
    The lords of Shame and Sin,
These all await the opening gate
    And haste to enter in.
Nay! Bar the threshold fast against
    That rebel spawn of Cain.
The gates wide fling to hail the King
    Whose right it is to reign.

No pomp and pageantry of power,
    No glint of shield or lance,
But hope and joy and righteousness
    Attend his meek advance.

Love is the banner over him,
    Peace is his gift to men.
Lift high your heads, ye New Year's gates,
    And let your King come in.

Romance, Limited

ROMANCE, LIMITED

Let us go to the end of the world, my love,
   To the end of the world today.
'Tis green beneath and blue above,
   And the long road calls "Away!"
The little white clouds are waving us on.
The year is at June, the day's at the dawn.
   Let us go to the end, and stay.

Forget the trivial things that were
   And the people we used to be.
There is nothing else in the world, I swear,
   But Love and you and me.
We will go to the end, and then go on
Till the stars are dead, or the gas is gone—
   But I *must* get home for tea.

A VALENTINE

That little thing called politics,
   Such small concerns as wealth,
Business and books and art and sport
   And food and even health—

These cannot hold my interest.
   I am not so prudential.
While these all have their use, no doubt,
   You are my one essential.

THE TIMID-BOLD LOVER

A delayed response to the following lines from Edmund Spenser's *An Hymn in Honour of Love* (c.1590)

> Then forth he casts in his unquiet thought,
> What he may do, her favour to obtaine;
> What brave exploit, what peril hardly wrought,
> What pleasant conquest, what adventurous paine,
> May please her best, and grace unto him gaine;
> He dreads no danger, nor misfortune feares;
> His faith, his fortune in his breast he beares.
> Witness Leander in the Euxine waves,
> And stout Aeneas in the Trojane fyre,
> Achilles pressing through the Phrygian glaives,
> And Orpheus, daring to provoke the yre
> Of damned fiends, to get his love retyre;
> For both through heaven and hell thou makest way
> To win them worship which to thee obey.

If only I were a rich man and you were a beggar maid,
  How gladly I would dower you with all my worldly
    wealth;
But you have plenty, and I have nought but a heart that's
    half afraid
  And a little gift of tinkling rhymes and not the best of
    health.

If I were a splendidly armoured knight and you were in
    vile duress,
  I'd storm the stoutest castle walls and valorous deeds
    I'd do;
But here in the city if I should try to save you from
    distress,
  I'd only make a fool of myself and perhaps embarrass
    you.

If you were cast in a seething sea, and I from the reeling
    deck
  Of a sinking craft beheld your plight, in spite of terrors
    grim
I'd plunge in the smother of foaming waves and save you
    from the wreck.
  But here we are upon dry land. Besides, I cannot swim.

So since I fit no hero's role and never can essay
  The noble deeds that better men would gladly do for
      you,
I give the nothing that I have, with what poor grace I
      may,
  Glad only that you do not need the things I cannot do.

NIGHT SONG

Dreams, sweet dreams,
  Come from the Master of sleep,
Lighten your load if it seems
  Too great, or the waters too deep.
  If the day has been gray and the bravest must weep,
May the night bring golden dreams.

Let a dream, sweet dream,
  Come as you count the sheep.
If the day is a bitter stream,
  Of night's mellow wine drink deep.
  The way by day is rough and steep,
So dream, sweet, dream.

FORGETTING

  I must remember to forget you, dear.
  When waking birds are twittering in the eaves,
  When the east glows and the lark rises
  And all the old familiar sweet surprises
  Of budding dawn come as the light grows clear,
  When morning's petals open and the day
  Bursts into bloom among the waiting leaves,
  I must remember to forget, I say.
  It were far easier to remember, yet—
  I must forget.

Tramping the shady path through the deep wood,
Resting upon a stone,
Feeling the zest of speed on the open road
And the motor's musical tone.
Uplifted by beauty, I must believe it good
To be alone.

A book on my knee, unread as the light grows pale;
The ripples' lisp at my feet;
The sibilant murmur of waves as the day winds fail
And the light and the darkness meet.
    (Day is a lover and night is a bride,
    Fated to live apart.
    But they meet at dawn and eventide.
    The world between them is wide—so wide—
    But it cannot prison the heart.)

It is not kind that the moon should come tonight
And sparkle upon the lake and silver the trees,
For I am forgetting, forgetting with all my might,
And the moon and the stars are made for memories.
But the moon is young—too young to stay up late,
And her slender sickle will sink if I patiently wait.

So I shall wait with a minimum
Of fruitless repining and regretting,
And then, though the effort strike me dumb,
Get back to my task of forgetting.

CHANCE

A moment later, a hurried pace,
    An instant's pause or the least delay,
And I had not met you face to face
    That well-remembered day.

For only one instant our pathways crossed,
   And in only one spot—we knew not where.
But the flower and fruit of life had been lost
   If I had not found you there.

Groping through boundless time and space
   By paths we could neither see nor miss,
Blindly we sought the trysting place
   And blundered into bliss.

One chance in a million. But all chance ends
   When kindly Chance such a chance discovers.
A moment before, we were less than friends;
   The next, we were more than lovers.

We kept a tryst we knew not of,
   A casual rendezvous with Fate,
With Life and Destiny and Love.
   Thank God, I came not late.

PYGMALION TO GALATEA

Wake, Galatea, wake! It cannot be
   You have not sensed the pressure of the hand
That stroked the yielding clay to symmetry.
   It must be that you feel and understand
How mounting ardor tempered every touch,
   How pride of skill was lost in tenderness,
Till at the last the sculptor's love was such
   That every chisel blow was a caress.

Wake, Galatea! Breathe, and look, and live.
   Marble thou wast; be now divinely human.
Nay, spirit thou wast, 'tis only flesh I give.
   With both, be now the incomparable woman.
Not as an artifact would I possess thee,
   Fruit of my toil, for keeping or for losing.
With lifted hands I liberate and bless thee.
   Mine is the maker's joy, thine the free choosing.

For, if some skill of mine in plastic art
  Has shaped the stone to beauty, if the strife
Of love to frame its object warms the heart
  Of marble till it flutters into life,
Your loveliness no less has quickened me,
  Waking what slumbered since my life began.
You, fresh created, hold creation's key.
  Sculptor I was; your love will make me man.

A LADY TAKES THE VEIL

(but not really)

Vain world, I here renounce
All thy crude pomps and shows.
The Devil cannot pounce
On me in this sweet close
Where virgin lilies spring
Beside the garden path,
And nones and vespers ring
To mollify God's wrath.

Flesh, thou canst charm me not—
Either my own or others.
Love, thou art well forgot.
Here pure devotion smothers
All fires of earthly passion—
Ah, fierce they were and blasting—
The while I meekly fashion
My soul with prayer and fasting.

Dear God, I hope *he* every day reflects
How pale I grow behind this convent door,
And that that other grieves if he suspects
I had been his if he had kissed once more.

DISTANCE, I

It is not parting from the friend I love
That gives me grief. For friendship, swift as light,
Stronger than death, by its own mystic might
Can span the miles and rocky barriers move.
We are not prisoners of time and space,
Bound to some little acre of green earth,
Vassals of Here and Now. With radiant mirth
Our hearts might leap the seas to close embrace.

But when I sit beside you, hand in hand,
Searching your eyes for some assuring sign
To tell me that you trust and understand,
Yet feel no touch or glance that answers mine—
Better with love a thousand leagues between
Than face to face yet hidden by that screen.

DISTANCE, II

I want you here, O love, I want you now.
What though my eager fancy paints a clear
And lovely image of your face most dear?
And what though memory echoes every vow
We've whispered each to each? What though I bow
In feigned submission, with pretended cheer
Biding the time until you shall be near?
I want you here, O love, I want you now.

I want you now, O love, I want you here.
I am no fleshless spirit of thin air
To feed on hopes and visions. But I peer
Into the distance, yearning in despair
To see your eyes, to touch your lips, your hair.
I want you now, O love, I want you here.

COULD THIS BE A VALENTINE?

(Recently discovered manuscript; author and addressee unknown;
authenticity doubtful)

Dai that every Lovour loves,
Dai of Heartes and Fleures and Douves,
What need hav I for such Occascioun
To speak the Wordes of sweete Persuascion?

Love, ever new but never straunge,
Chaunges not while Seasouns chaunge.
So love me long and love me hard,
For I am trulie youres.
                                   —Bernard

GO ON, REMEMBERING

If I shall pause a while beside the way—
  A little while to sleep and dream and rest
  And find some wiser word, some fresher zest
To sound a happier note another day,—
Do not thou halt, good comrade, when I fall,
  Or falter when thou dost not hear me sing.
The distance beckons. Far horizons call.
  Do thou go on—go on, remembering.

The past is ours, secure from chance and change.
  Buoyant and brave as now, go on, regretting
  Naught that is gone, naught fearing, naught forgetting.
The future shall be neither harsh nor strange.
For, spite of all that life or death may bring,
  I shall go on with you—remembering.

LOVE AND LIFE

Oh, Love and Death go ever in hand,
For poison lurks within the magic cup
Which love to thirsty lips is lifting up;
And those who tread the heavenly heights must stand

63

Upon a dizzy verge. Love's stern command
Summons to battle, wounds, and sudden death;
No languorous whisper borne on perfumed breath,
But ringing call to dare, by sea and land.

Yet love brings every gift of joy and grace,
Lightens the darkness, gives new life for old,
And touches all things with her mystic wand,
Making a temple every common place,
Like Midas turning all base things to gold,
For Love and Life go ever hand in hand.

PLATONIC—PLUS

I do not love you, dear—I mean
    As Romeo loved Juliet.
I clearly am no Montague,
    And you, thank heaven, no Capulet.

If I should love as Anthony
    Paolo, Launcelot, and Troilus
Loved Cleo, Frances, Guinevere
    And Cressida, 't would spoil us.

I do not love you, darling, thus.
    You must not trust a word I say
If ever, tempted, I should swear
    I love you in their ardent way.

I truly love your mind, heart, soul,
    Your thirst for truth, your sense of beauty,
Your warm sincerity, your firm
    Grasp upon honor and on duty.

I prize your quick intelligence;
    And, being male and wholly human,
I do not overlook the fact
    You are a very lovely woman.

RED ROSES

I brought her red roses,
    But she wore a yellow dress.
They were lovely, perfect posies,
    Yet they only gave distress.
'Twas disaster, nothing less,
For the deed too well discloses
    I'm the kind of man, I guess,
Who always brings red roses
    To match a yellow dress.

To have the best intentions
    In the heart is not enough,
For you just provoke dissensions
    If your technique is too rough.
If anyone supposes
    He can please without finesse—
Remember, all she knows is
That I brought her red roses
    When she wore a yellow dress.

MARE NOSTRUM

You walked beside me, dearest, yesterday,
    When those who met me thought I went alone,
    Out through the gate of Rome, where every stone
Is half alive, sleeping and dreaming—nay,
Waking at times to bid the traveler stay
    To share its dream on such an afternoon,
    To feel the sun and wait the rising moon
And watch the ghosts go down the Appian Way.

These ghosts walked not with me. But as I strode
    Over a hill, came from the shining west
    The gleam of sun on water, and I guessed—
Rather than saw—the sea where galleys rode

Once to the port of Rome, burdened with load
  Of precious plunder from the scattered isles.
  Conquered from east to west a thousand miles,
"Our sea" they called it in their haughty mode.

But you and I, love, have a western sea,
  Ours without conquest, by diviner right—
  At morn a crystal-sapphire sea; at night
A star-flecked sea of purple mystery
Where, homeward bound, sail many an argosy
  Of dream-hopes we have launched upon its tide.
  So every sea-glimpse brings you to my side,
And yesterday, unseen, you walked with me.

WORDS ONLY?

Words only for your birthday? Words, words, words!
And what are words, mere words? "Yet words do well
When he who speaks them pleases her who hears"—
As Shakespeare said. These limping lines may tell
Of earnest wishes for your present joy
And lively hopes, on this your natal day,
For future growth in wisdom and in grace.
May you have eager zest for work and play,
Live under Truth's command and Beauty's spell,
Buoyant and sensitive, serious and gay.

TSENG TZU ON LOTUS-BUD

(Chung Ni is a Chinese title for Confucius.
Tseng Tzu was one of his famous disciples.)

Chung Ni sit down.
Tseng Tzu stand humble.
"Master, what think
'Bout gals?" he mumble.

"Just one in thousand
Worth a rap.
Be realistic.
Don't be sap."

"Don't be big fool,"
Chung Ni reply.
"Nobody know—
Not even I.

Tseng Tzu bow low:
"That one, she mine.
You take nine hun-
Dred ninety-nine.

"Man know too much
'Bout *genus* woman,
He never know
One piece girl human.

"My Lotus-Bud,
She different story;
Not just in female
Category—

"Tall, short, dark, light,
Faded and fresh, all—
She just herself,
Unique and special."

Chung Ni stand up.
He swallow pride.
"You wiser man
Than me," he sighed.

THERE IS A LOVE

There is a love that asks for everything,
    And will not be denied.
It comes with banners like a conquering king
    To claim a vanquished bride.
Its boasts are great; its gifts no less;
But all it wants is to possess;
For half of it is selfishness
    And half of it is pride.

There is a love that comes in suppliant guise
    And lingers at the door,
Tapping so gently and so beggar-wise
    But tapping o'er and o'er.
Its strength is in its utter need,
A heart that breaks and hands that bleed;
But, meek and patient, it will plead
    For more and ever more.

There is a love that asks no recompense,
    Only some little sign
That it may dare to stand without offense
    And worship at its shrine.
What gifts it has, it is its joy to bring
And give them without stint or bargaining,
Content if it may only serve and sing—
    And such a love is mine.

Trivialia et Frivola

THE BONG OF WONG

("The Bong of Wong, chieftain of one of the
largest tribes of headhunters in Assam, has de-
clared war on Japan."—News item.)

O lift a song
To the Bong of Wong,
With his two-handed kris and his blue sarong.
As a hunter of heads he is stout and strong,
And the hunting of heads can't be far wrong
When the heads he is hunting now belong
To the ruffians who looted fair Hongkong.
So sound the trumpet and beat the gong.
It won't be long,
It won't be long,
Now we've enlisted the Bong of Wong,
The truculent Bong
Of succulent Wong,
The headhunting Bong
Of Wong.

REPORT AT EIGHTY-FIVE

I have work that I like, and get paid for,
Yet plenty of leisure, I find,
To use for what leisure is made for,
The improvement of heart and of mind.

My banker says, "Decently solvent."
 My doctor says, "Sound, top to toe."
I have friends true and tried,
And my foes have all died,
 So my *status* is practically *quo*.

THIS LITTLE WORLD

One evening in a Pullman car
 I met a man of pleasant mien.
We talked of topics near and far,
 Of where we'd been and what we'd seen.
Before an hour had passed, we found
 He knew my cousin in St. Paul.
He smiled and said, with thought profound,
 "How small the world is after all."

On boats and cars, where throngs are dense,
 On mountain tops, at far trails' ends,
With unforeseen coincidence
 I meet old friends, or friends of friends.
I'm glad to see them, but I dread
 Those words so unoriginal,
Those words which always must be said,
 "How small the world is after all."

I'd like to go abroad again
 And visit places seen before,
But some day in the Madeleine,
 Or in St. Gotthard Tunnel's bore,
In Moscow, Rome, or Guadalup',
 I'd hear the friendly, foolish call
Of some well-meaning nincompoop,
 "How small the world is after all."

And so I dare not travel now.
  I've lost my zest for foreign shores.
No strangers will I meet, I vow.
  I shun my fellowmen as bores.
For everywhere, on land or sea,
  Some blithering idiot will bawl,
In quaint surprise and stupid glee,
  "How small the world is after all."

ARS POETICA

I

Sometimes from out the boundless blue
There comes a fluttering line or two
Of singing verse, all wild and shy
As creatures from an alien sky.

Unsought they come, through no design
Or clever artifice of mine,
And through my open casement dance,
Blown by some happy wind of chance;

Or stealthily through my open door
They slip, to visit and explore,
Seeking a warmer, friendlier place
Than the chill realm of outer space.

And then, if I keep out of sight
And very still and neither write
Nor speak nor think, except to be
Aware that these have come to me,

And wait with hospitable heart
Till others come or these depart,
And let my soul in silence thrill
But bid my clumsy tongue be still,—

It may be, if the fates are kind,
These timid visitants will find
My room, in spite of desk and book,
A homely, hospitable nook.

Then forth they fare on hastening wing
And flocks of tuneful comrades bring,
Till the wild, friendly, heavenly throng
Have filled my chamber with their song.

Then quick, my pen! With conscience light,
With harmless plagiarism write
Each thrilling note, each glowing word—
The song I have not made but heard.

ARS POETICA

II

Not always does verse come unsought
And sing to me, for some is bought
At cost of labor hard enough,
The more the toil, the worse the stuff.

Sometimes I think I have a thought
That must be clothed in garments wrought
Of rare and lofty imagery
And bodied forth in poetry.

First, to decide which rhythm is best,
Dactyl, trochee, or anapest.
Are triolets or sonnets neater,
Or this four-foot iambic meter?

(Whichever one I choose, I know
I shall regret it, for a flow
Of lines will come that suit the theme
But will not fit the rhythmic scheme.)

That problem solved, I must select
Some rhyming words. (A poem's wretched
Unless one has the skill sublime
To shun end words that will not rhyme.)

And so, by industry immense,
By aid of works of reference,
With books of rhymes and synonyms,
With epics, elegies, and hymns

To furnish me allusions pat,
Poetic figures and all that,—
With hammer, saw, and studied plan,
I build some verse as best I can.

Alas, the poor pathetic thing
Can neither walk, nor speak, nor sing.
The thought I *thought* I thought, pale-browed
It lies within its flowery shroud.

Choked by the words I wrapped around it,
It died before I really found it,
And in the garments of its birth
I must commit it, earth to earth.

SUMMARY AND MORAL

However bad my unsought verse,
The things I *make* are always worse.

SATTOMON

(A lakeside cabin in the Indiana Dunes)

Deep in the dunes stands Sattomon.
  Old Indian name, from its sound.
But the dwindling tribe has long since gone
  To the happy hunting ground.
Snow unbroken in gully and glade;
Bare oaks marching in gaunt parade

Over the hills; and a lake of jade
  Full of mystery.

Like friendly beasts the north winds roar,
  But they mean no serious harm,
And behind a stout and sheltering door
  The hearth is bright and warm.
The sparks fly up; the kettle sings;
The smoke spins delicate spirals and rings;
An easy chair and books and things weave a potent charm.

O good green cabin! There's nothing so sweet,
  When the work of the week is done,
As the peace of a snug and safe retreat
  In the dunes from Sat. to Mon.

MAY MORNING AT SATTOMON

At eight o'clock a fog like silk
  Wrapped in the cabin, wrapped out the world.
At nine o'clock it was white as milk,
  But every leaf was gemmed and pearled
Where the wild grape crept to the cabin door,
  Where the black oaks tapped at the windowpane.
At ten, the white silk drapery tore
  Into ribbons that glistened like sunlit rain.

And then the ribbons were shredded to lace,
  And the lace dissolved to a luminous gauze,
    Revealing, enhancing
    The witching, entrancing,
    Slow languorous dancing
Of shimmering waves as with sinuous grace,
    Retreating, advancing,
  They softly and lazily moved without pause,
Reluctant, yet seeking the shore's embrace.

This is the meeting of hills and sea,
  Of full-blown day and the budding dawn.
This is the marvel and mystery
  Of a foggy May morning at Sattomon.

A KODAK IN THE MOUNTAINS

(A rainy morning in Glacier National Park)

Press the button, tourist,
  Click—click—click!
That's the way to get the sights
  Easy, cheap, and quick.
There's the Blackfoot Glacier (*Click*).
There's a grazing wild goat (*Quick*).
F.16 will do the trick.
  Click—click—click!

Rain in silver ribbons
  Is spangling the spruce.
All the rills are chattering.
  The clouds are flying loose.
One could dream enchanted dreams.
Or shout with joy beside the streams,
But—rotten days for snaps, it seems,
  So what's the bally use?

Leagues of granite grandeur
  Challenging the sky;
Mysteries and glories
  Of stark immensity.
But there's no time for wonder (*Click*).
Press the button, tourist (*Quick*).
Have them printed, dull or slick.
  Photos never lie.

74

KALYPSIS

(The following is the result [apparently acciden-
tal] of reading William Empson's brilliant *Seven
Types of Ambiguity,* in which the sixth type, which
is regarded as having great possibilities, is one in
which the author does not know what the poem
means and can only hope that some reader may
find a meaning in it—though it will rather spoil
the fun if one does.)

Never may any credo have the scope,
    The tangible dimensions, or the passion
To mediate the gulf 'twixt doubt and hope,
    Or integrate the stresses, in my fashion.
    The knife-edged bridge that cuts a haggard gash in
The symbiotic complex of each fraction
Weakens or frustrates every interaction.
Intensive, libratory, and tenacious,
    The encounter stipples with its throbbing unction
The lost millennium, blindly sequacious,
    That tartens with its acid every function.
    And so, without remorse, without compunction,
I greet the cyclothymic telegnosis
And pour libations—roses, roses, roses.

A LITERARY EDITOR'S HOLIDAY

(A rhymed review of *The Saga of Cap'n John Smitty*)[1]

This facile concoction of legend and myth
Recounting the exploits of Cap'n John Smitty
Is not such a welter of vacant hilarity
As some may suppose. Kindly note the disparity
Between the light-hearted uproarious spirit
In which Mr. Ward splits his sides (or comes near it)
By howling, as though 'twere a college prep school,

---

[1]The title in full is "The Saga of Cap'n John Smith" (and who cares if the things
didn't happlen), by Christopher Ward, who confounds all the scholars. Harper & Row,
publishers. $2.00.

The "Brek-ek-ek-ex" yell "Dear Old Stamboul,"
And the satire, quite sober though spoken in jest,
Which he hurls at the follies and faults of the West.
The Boston police and the *censor librorum*,
How he does larrup 'em, scorch 'em and score 'em.
He wars against war. He attacks the police
For breaking the laws in preserving the peace.
He punctures the pretense of judges whose game
Is to confiscate liquor and guzzle the same.
He runs to the rescue of Sacco-Vanzetti,
Derides over-zealous red-hunters, and yet he
Includes some flag-waving of excellent quality
Mixed with this melange of legend and jollity,
And pours on the British satirical mirth
For bragging and swaggering and grabbing the earth.
As to Smith, there are episodes patently mythical,
Yet the less they are likely the more they are Smithical.
I don't like to question a gentleman's word,
But sometimes I doubt if they ever occurred.

The Duke's
Christmas Pageant

and

Il Poverello

THE DUKE'S
CHRISTMAS PAGEANT

FOREWORD

THIS CHRISTMAS PLAY was designed to be given, and has been given many times, in a church. It can be presented in any place where there is room for the action and where enough people will enter into it with a proper mingling of reverence and gaiety.

It is in three parts: a dinner, a series of tableaux, which may loosely be called a "mystery play," with accompanying verse and music; and such subsequent revelries and merrymaking as are suitable to the season and congenial to the tastes of the company. The first will naturally be in the dining room, the second in the sanctuary or auditorium, the third in whatever place is most convenient.

The time is conceived to be Christmas Eve in the year of our Lord 1000; the place, a duke's castle far away. The chief characters are: the Duke and Duchess (perhaps the pastor and his wife), the Master of the Revels (who also becomes the reader of the text), a Herald, the Chief Troubadour (tenor soloist), a band of Singers (the church choir), and a Company of Strolling Players costumed to present the tableaux. Since the setting is medieval, it helps if many of the people were some approximation to medieval costume, but none should be embarrassed by coming in modern garb, as most of them usually do.

Certain formalities should be observed, but these can be improvised. The most convenient method is to have the main company of diners seated at the tables before the Duke and Duchess enter with their attendants. As these enter, there should be a flourish of trumpets and the Herald with a sonorous voice annonunces the (make-believe) title of each Knight and Lady. When all are in their places, a Canticle of Thanksgiving is sung, and the banquet is served. During the service carols may be sung by the band of singers or by a group of children.

When all have eaten, a character garbed as a monk reminds the Duke that the season calls for holy thoughts as well as merriment and feasting. The Master of the Revels informs him that by chance a Company of Strolling Players has arrived and asks permission to present certain scenes from a mystery play appropriate to the season. Permission granted, the entire assembly proceeds to the sanctuary in orderly fashion, following the Duke and Duchess and their attendants. "O Come, All Ye Faithful" may be sung as a processional hymn. Others who were not at the dinner will already be seated. In the sanctuary the Singers take their place on one side, the Master of the Revels at a reading desk on the other, where they can be heard but scarcely seen by the audience in the darkened room. The Singers may sing "The First Noel."

THE TABLEAUX

Prologue

God greet ye, gentle folk, both great and small,
Who have come hither at the Herald's call,
And give you joy that is most meet to be
Upon the eve of Christ's nativity.
Let it be known to those who have not shared
The feast our liege's bounty had prepared

That we are here as those who celebrate
The advent of God's glory incarnate
When just ten centuries have passed away
Since broke the dawn of the first Christmas Day.
It is the end of one millennium.
The second—and a better—is to come.
But if into our carols or our rhyme
There creeps some flavor of a later time,
It is a sign his kingdom—potent, vast—
Commands the future as it rules the past.

Now, while ye rightly revel and rejoice,
Give ear, and gladly, to a solemn voice
Whose tuneful homilies do you to wit
How men in drear and dreadful dark did sit
Till came, upon a midnight, one who brought
The saving light to those all sore distraught.
Soon by our players' art shall ye have sight
Of what befell upon that holy night.
But hear ye first how, by the prophet's word,
Came promise of great comfort from the Lord
When David's throne was empty of a king
And captive Jewry languished sorrowing.

Then shall be sung, by a tenor voice, "Comfort Ye My People"
and "Every Valley Shall Be Exalted' from Handel's *Messiah.*

King Herod's Court

The prophet's voice was drowned in blood and tears
And swallowed in the tumult of the years.
Full half a thousand years have passed, and still
Has God delayed his promise to fulfill.
In long procession through the centuries
Have marched the empires. Persians and Chaldees
Have hurled the thundering chariots of their wrath
O'er shattered lands from Nineveh to Gath.

The Macedonian stripling, drunk with power,
With slaughter filled his brief and bloody hour.
These ruthless conquerors, in dire sequence,
Have ruled the world by craft and violence.
In violence and craft they put their trust,
Rose, flourished, fell, and turned to acrid dust
Ground fine by Roman feet and blown aside
By the high wind of Roman power and pride.
Now great Augustus rules a docile earth
Taught quietness by fear. And now the birth
Of a new Golden Age is the report
Of Virgil, flattering poet of the court.
But force and hate still hold their ancient sway
While men grope blindly for a better way.
Rome lords it from the rivers to the sea,
But petty kinglets flaunt their pageantry
And hold their mimic courts in pomp and pride
With neither power to rule nor skill to guide,
As unsubstantial as the glittering foam
Flecking the billowed ocean might of Rome.

King Herod is Judea's king—
A gilded king, a guilty king,
A crafty, cruel, tinsel thing
    With a fair queen by his side.
His scepter is of proper gold,
His crown is rubies, pearl, and gold,
But his hand is heavy, his heart is cold,
    And he is weary-eyed.
With all his slaves and dancing girls,
His supple knaves and prancing girls,
And all his diamonds and pearls,
    And royal rank beside,
He is a pitiable thing—
A cruel but a timid king
Who fears the coming gentle King
    Whose meekness shames his pride.

First Tableau: King Herod's Court. During the tableau the organ or stringed instruments may play music of oriental character. After it the Singers may sing "Lo! How a Rose E'er Blooming" and "The Morning Stars on High."

The Annunciation

The times are ripe. Too great for lips of seer
The word earth waits and heaven stoops to hear.
None other than an angel, Gabriel,
Shall bring first tidings of Immanuel.
Bethink ye 'tis the high day of the spring
When lilies bloom and every fowl doth sing;
When night and day unite in equal measure
To dower the virgin earth with vernal treasure.
Now shall ye see how heaven's messenger,
All shining from God's presence, brought to her,
The wedded maiden, word that she should bear
A child than stars more bright, than moon more fair.

Second Tableau: The Annunciation. During the tableau the organ will play "Joy to the World." After it the Singers will sing "Though Thou Art Now an Infant Small" and "Jesus Meek and Mild."

The Nativity

There is both warmth and light, as you shall see,
Upon the night of Christ's nativity.
Winter to summer turns, and night to morn,
When Christ, the Everlasting Light, is born.

Third Tableau: The Nativity. During the tableau a quartette will sing "Silent Night" and "Shepherds, Shake off Your Drowsy Sleep."

The Shepherds

While simple shepherds watched their silly sheep
In snowy fields, there came to break their sleep

A heavenly messenger, who said to them:
"A child is born this night in Bethlehem."
Then sang a choir of angels in the sky:
"Peace among men, glory to God Most High."

The shepherds were many who lay that night
Guarding their flocks from danger and fright.
   The angels sang—a host of them.
The dogs were restless and sniffed and whined,
And the men were weary, and little inclined
   To leave their beds were most of them.

So some but dreamed of following
When they heard in their sleep the angels sing,
   And stirred in their slumber and slept again.
Some of them wakened and partly rose
But shivered to feel the winds and the snows
   And back to their blankets crept again.

But a few leaped up and followed the song
That came in the night and stayed not long.
   If the drowsy lingered, small blame to them.
But those who heard, and woke, and went
Made the frost and the snow a sacrament,
   And the world was never the same to them.

With wondering joy they rose and hastened down
To make their pilgrimage to David's town,
To greet the Child low-cradled in a stall
And hail on humble knees the Lord of all.

Fourth Tableau: The Shepherds. During the tableau the Singers may sing "God Rest You Merry, Gentlemen" and another carol.

The Wise Men

In Orient lands, where wealth and wisdom dwelt,
Yet people most in ignorant worship knelt
To pray to God-knows-who for God-knows-what,
Three men remembered what the rest forgot.

Sages were they, who knew the sacred lore
Of all the generations gone before;
And kings also, each in his own degree,
Enthroned in power and robed in majesty.
Reading the secrets that the stars had told,
They came with myrrh and frankincense and gold,
The tribute of their kingdoms to the King
Low-lying in a manger's cradle-ing.
Wisdom pays homage unto innocence
And power to poverty does reverence.
Behold them, hither guided by the star,
The Magi—Caspar, Melchior, Balthazar.

Fifth Tableau: The Wise Men. During the tableau the Singers will sing "We Three Kings of Orient Are" and, in preparation for the final tableau, "Hark, the Herald Angels Sing" and "Glory to God."

The Angels

Shepherds have brought their humble adoration,
The rich and great their homage and oblation.
Some higher note of praise must still be sounded
For him whose kingdom over all is bounded
By heights of heaven and hell's blackest rage,
By dawn of time and by the endless age.
Sing, heavenly choir, angelic host, who first
Announced the newborn Prince of Peace and burst
The silence of the centuries to sing
The coming of a meek and conquering King.
Sing once again, while men rejoice to see
The light that shines from Christ's nativity.

Sixth Tableau: The Host of Angels, and ensemble. The "Hallelujah Chorus" will be sung during the tableau. At the end, the lights on the scene are gradually dimmed and the house lights brightened. The Master of the Revels, who has been the unseen reader of the lines, appears upon the platform and speaks the Epilogue.

Epilogue

The play is done. The angel vision pales
Into the common light. But naught avails
The Hallelujah and the song of peace
If, ere the echoes of the anthem cease,
And ere the music of their praise is still,
Men shall forget their message of goodwill.
Let swords be sheathed, harsh words and thoughts
   grow mild.
So shall ye honor best the heaven-sent Child.

Let mirth abound. And may God give you grace,
And you, good people, who have made this place
The better by your presence, lord and thrall,
Right Merrie Christmas. To the upper hall
The Duke and all his guests will now repair
To see what cheer in readiness is there.
The night is young. Hours are as wisely spent
In festal joy as on deep thought intent.
Come all who will and join the merriment.

THE REVELS

During a recessional, played on the organ or by stringed
instruments, the Duke and his Attendants will leave the
chapel, followed by all the people, and proceed to whatever apartment has been prepared for the further festivi-
ties, there to engage in suitable and seasonable revelries.
For this part of the pageant there is no script.

IL POVERELLO—A PLAY OF ST. FRANCIS

(acknowledgments to Laurence Housman, whose
Little Plays of St. Francis suggested the general
pattern of this play, but who is followed only in
transforming the *Fioretti's* "fierce wolf of Agobio,"
which Francis is said to have converted, into the
robber, Lupo.)

PROLOGUE

There was a time—of course this must have been long
ago—when ambition, avarice, and pride made men un-
brotherly. Generous impulses were checked by fear. The
rich feared they might become poor; the poor feared they
might starve; the strong feared to be merciful lest they
be deemed weak. But always there were some who did
not fear. These were the valiant few for whom the love
of God meant love for the lowly, the loathsome, the
erring, and the hostile. This love gave them an uncon-
querable courage and a power that has outlasted empires.

Such was Giovanni Francesco Bernardone, who gave up
his wealthy home, easy living and social popularity to
become the Little Poor Man of Assisi and servant of all.
About him gathered a group who became the Little
Brothers of the Poor. Their winsome ways won many to
new understanding of the possibility of brotherhood among
men.

87

The time is about the year 1200. The place is the Italian town of Assisi. The scene is in open country near enough to the town for numbers of townsfolk and peasants to be passing along the road, and far enough for the town's lepers to be collected there and for robbers to haunt the region.

The characters are:

Francesco Bernardone (St. Francis)

Brothers Leo, Rufino, and Angelo (later called the Three Companions)

Brother Junipero

Rudolfo, Francis' former rival and enemy, now a leper

Four other lepers

Lupo, a robber, and four members of his band

Two beggars, a youth with a lute and one singing, 3 or 4 young men of fashion, townspeople, and peasants on the road.

It is late afternoon. The light is bright, but the shadows are lengthening. Two beggars sit by the road, one with a wooden bowl, the other too weak to beg. Townspeople and peasants pass along the road in both directions, some with bundles—a roll of blankets, chickens tied together by the feet, a wine jar, etc. The beggar whines for alms and holds up his bowl. Two or three toss copper coins into it. Two youths stroll by, one with a lute, one singing.

BEGGER: *(whining more loudly):* Alms, alms, good sirs! A gift to the poor is a gift to God.

SINGER: Hold, hold, Paolo. This croaker puts me off the key.

LUTE PLAYER: How like a dark cloud in a bright sky is this beggar's whine against a song of love.

SINGER: A cloud! Nay. A cloud at least is silent. It is the croaking of a raven against the song of larks.

LUTE PLAYER: Come! If this raven must croak, let me set his croaking to music. *(Strikes minor chords stridently as the beggar continues his appeal in a harsh voice.)*

SINGER: Peace, Paolo! Your lute has no notes to match his stale lament. Give me the pitch again.

BEGGER: Alms, young masters! A copper coin. Some day you may be friendless.

SINGER: Then will we keep our friendly coin against that unfriendly day.

LUTE PLAYER: Sing, Rinaldo, sing! *(He strikes up a lively air and they pass on, singing. Some peasants pass. Then a group of young men.)*

FIRST: What play we had today!

THIRD: I had only to whisper to the dice and they did my bidding.

SECOND: And mine! Did you not see? When the stake was small, they let it go.

FIRST: Yes, and when my opponent let his lie to double, once and again, ha, ha! the wise dice saw and took all.

THIRD: We shall celebrate in Assisi tonight.

BEGGER: Alms, my lords, alms! A gift to the poor is a—

SECOND *(tossing a silver coin):* Here, ugly face, stop thy howling. With this thou canst rest thy throat for a week; aye, and wet it too.

BEGGER: Silver! God bless thee, generous master. A gift to the—

SECOND: Rest thy throat, I told thee. And thank not me. The silver cost me nothing.

THIRD: Thank that rash youth of Perugia who played with it, if thou canst find him.

FIRST: He will be sitting beside thee with a beggar's bowl before the month is out, if he make not better friends with Lady Luck.

> *The youths pass on down the road, chattering inaudibly. The shadows grow longer. Francis enters, followed by Leo, Rufino, Angelo and Junipero. The beggar is silent as they approach. As Francis pauses, the beggar raises his bowl, as from habit, looks at them and at the silver coin in his hand, and lowers the bowl.*

FRANCIS: How is it, brother? Hast thou need of nothing?

BEGGER: I have a piece of silver. Tonight my belly shall be filled.

FRANCIS: *Thy* belly only? Has then thy friend silver also?

BEGGER: Friend? I have no friend. *(Glancing at the beggar beside him)* This is no friend of mine. Let him beg for himself.

FRANCIS: No friend? Then thou art poorer than I thought. Here, the air grows chill and night comes on. Thy coat is thin, brother. The wind will make shrill music on its shredded strings, but such music warms neither the heart nor the ribs. *(Taking off his robe and placing it on the beggar's shoulders with a caressing gesture)* Do thy warm office as faithfully to thy new master as thou hast to me. *(Starts off, then turns and adds:)* If thou seest one with a coat worse than thine, thy heart will tell thee what to do.

90

Francis and his company pass on slowly. The beggar looks after them, then at his fellow, hesitates a moment, then takes off the cloak and drapes it over the other's shoulders. Brother Leo, looking back, sees the act. He runs back and gives his cloak to the first beggar, and hurries to catch the others before they shall notice his absence.

FRANCIS *(without turning his head):* Thou hast done wisely, Brother Leo. How soft grows the evening air.

A company of lepers have taken their place at one side, some distance from the road. It is the place where they are supposed to be confined. They are quarreling. One snatches a bowl from another and dashes it down.

FIRST LEPER: Heaven rot thee, foul lump of corruption that thou art. *(Dashes bowl to the ground.)*

SECOND LEPER *(whining):* Yesterday thou didst steal my portion of bread that the guard brought. Now thou dost break my bowl.

THIRD LEPER: And what then, vile one? The bread was mouldy, as thou art, and the bowl was cracked, like thy brain.

FIRST LEPER: Thou art as good as dead already. What need of bread and bowl? Go hide thyself.

A guard approaches with a new leper to be added to the colony. The leper has a cord around his neck, attached to one end of a pole the other end of which is held by the guard, who thrusts him violently into the group, releasing the cord by a flip as he does so. The new leper has clothing

91

much better than the rags of the others, and a bag of food. He falls on his knees in an attitude of despair.

NEW LEPER: Come quickly, swift and merciful death, for cruel living death has already laid hold on me.

The other lepers pounce upon him, strip off his outer garments and snatch them from one another, and make off with his bag of food, quarreling over it. The lepers jibe at the newcomer and quarrel among themselves.

SECOND LEPER: This is thy fee for admission to this fair company.

NEW LEPER: Let go, swine.

FIRST LEPER: Give me that tunic. It does not match thy complexion.

SECOND LEPER: Thou hast no business with white bread. Thou art a leper now. Dost thou not know? A leper—

THIRD LEPER: Look! Here comes again he who came to us yesterday.

SECOND LEPER: He said he would return, but who could believe a thing so incredible?

FIRST LEPER: It was a miracle that he came once, but to come twice—

FRANCIS: Brothers, did you not know that I would come?

FIRST LEPER: "Brothers"? To lepers?

SECOND LEPER: We are not brothers even to one another.

THIRD LEPER: There is more hatred here than between borrower and lender, or between master and slave.

SECOND LEPER: We have nothing left but hatred. Call you us "brothers"?

FRANCIS: Why not? Cut off from the world, why must you also cut yourselves off from one another? You are bound to this place, but your minds may be free if you will. Your hearts may be free from bitterness as you are free to rejoice in the sun which as freely shines on you as on any, and to feel the breeze that freely blows upon you. If you would serve one another, you would love; and he who loves is free. *(To Rudolfo, who has sat at one side without speaking, his face masked and his feet bound up.)* Brother, your feet are dusty with the long day. May I wash them?

FIRST LEPER *(in tone of horror)*: "Dusty!" Poverello, his feet are no longer feet, as his face is no longer a face.

RUDOLFO: You would wash my feet? Do you know me?

FRANCIS *(half humorously)*: It is true that thy mask somewhat obscures—

RUDOLFO *(lifting the mask)*: Look then, if there remains aught to see. *(Francis starts in recognition.)* 'Tis so, I am Rudolfo, thy rival in the days of thy wealth; thy enemy in the time of thy popularity. What sayest thou now to washing my feet? Ha!

FRANCIS: Rufino, bring water. *(He unbinds and washes Rudolfo's feet and wipes them with a towel he carries tucked in the cord at his waist.)*

RUDOLFO: So may my sins be washed away. My hatred is already gone.

FRANCIS: If thy hatred is gone, then have thy sins gone with it. *(Rising)* Come, brothers, we must return toward the city. The night has fallen. *(It has grown dusk.)* But I would that we might find Brother Lupo and his robbers ere they do themselves grievous injury by robbing more travelers.

BROTHER JUNIPERO: I am but a fool, Father, but I know that wise men do not seek Lupo and his fellows either at noon or at nightfall.

FRANCIS: And why seek we not the robbers? Are they not men?

LEO: 'Tis not a week since they were robbing and killing in the streets of Assisi, and beat off the guard. Thou knowest Lupo swore he would either flog or hang thee for saying thou wouldst bring him into the city without a guard.

FRANCIS: Lupo knows well that I cannot bring him in unless he comes willingly.

JUNIPERO: Those shadows! There by the rocks! What are they? Men! *(Sinking down in terror while the others shrink back)* Oh, it is Lupo, the Wolf.

FRANCIS: Why, so I think it is. How fortunate! Now he can return with us to the city.

LEO: Return with us! Thou canst not believe that he will go—

JUNIPERO *(hotly)*: While the guard is scouring the byways for him, and a price is set on his head?

FRANCIS: Who can say? Perhaps no one has ever asked him to return to the lawful ways of men. Brother Lupo!

Francis' friendly call is smothered in an onslaught by the robbers as they rush upon the little party and bind Francis with a rope.

FRANCIS: This is kindly done, Brother Lupo. I thank thee for it. Now that thee and I are both prisoners in bonds, we can talk as comrades.

LUPO: I bound? Mad monk, what meanest thou? I am free—free from the law; free from the meddling of men; free from the city I hate. I am free to go where I please and do what I will—even to cut out thy bold tongue that boasted to take me bound into the city.

FRANCIS: Not bound, Brother Lupo. God forbid. Now thou art bound, but thou must be free before thou canst return to Assisi.

LUPO: Thou speakest in riddles. How am I bound?

FRANCIS: Bound by thy own hatred and by other men's fear of thee. There lies the city. The lights in its windows tell where there are happy homes. Friendship and the warm glow of love are there. Women smile and children laugh. Joy and peace are over all. But is there one home that thou couldst enter and be welcomed? Is there one friendly circle thou canst join without casting upon it the blight of fear? Thou hast built about thyself a wall of violence and hate that shuts thee away from the hearts of men. Thou hast riveted upon thine own ankles chains that keep thee from walking with them. Yes, Brother Lupo, thou and I are both in bonds, but thine are the more grievous. I would I might loose thee from them, for love has brought me here for no other purpose.

LUPO: Thou art a brave fellow to speak thus to me. I will loose thee from thy bonds. (*He cuts the ropes.*) But why should I love Assisi? True, I was born there. She was my mother, but she cast me out. When I was in want, she showed me no charity. In my heedless youth, when I was at fault, she showed me no mercy. When I was wronged, she gave me no justice. If now I rob her rich and despise her poor and if I put terror into their hearts, have I not a right? What is there left to me but hate?

FRANCIS: Love is left for thee, Brother Lupo. There is as much of it in the world as ever. Thou canst not bring on night by shutting thy eyes. Neither canst thou put men in bondage to thy vengeance, and thyself remain free from their fear of thee or from thy own hatred. Come, brother, be free! Leave thy prison. Its gates are open.

95

LUPO: I would such freedom were for me.

FRANCIS. Go down with us into the city and begin again to learn the liberty of brotherhood.

The bells of Assisi are heard in the distance.

LUPO *(to his companions):* Comrades, do you hear? Do you dare? Shall we go with Il Poverello?

A ROBBER: Master, we have followed thee in many desperate adventures, but none perhaps as desperate as this.

LUPO: The more desperate, the better it suits the temper of brave fellows like you. Often have we risked our lives to rob men and make them hate us as we hated them.

FRANCIS: Risk once more to make them love thee.

LUPO: We go tonight upon the adventure of Brotherhood. Lead on!

The bells, which have continued to sound indistinctly, are heard more clearly as the Brothers and the Robbers move off in mingled company toward Assisi following Francis and Lupo.